With Open Hands

Poems by Phillip Emanuel Frost Bounds

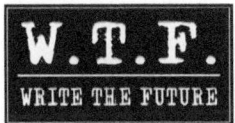

Write the Future   Jump Start ArtKC
Kansas City, MO   Kansas City, MO

Copyright (c) Phillip Bounds, 2019
First Edition 1 3 5 7 9 10 8 6 4 2
ISBN: 978-1-950380-27-5
LCCN: 2019900090

Design, edits and layout: Jason Ryberg
Cover and title page image: Phillip Bounds
The cover image is of the World War I Museum
and the title page image is of a Gibson Hummingbird.
Author photo: Erin Lorene Photography
All rights reserved. No part of this publication may be reproduced or transmitted in any form or by any means, electronic or mechanical, including photocopying, recording or by info retrieval system, without prior written permission from the author.

Acknowledgments

I would like to thank Eric Stephenson, my Comp II instructor, who taught me to love poetry and introduced me to T. S. Eliot, without which I would not have later started to write poetry. I am truly grateful to Sharon Eiker for making a place for new poetic voices by hosting poetry open mics in Kansas City including the Writer's Place, and Blue Monday; without her push and the help of JumpstartArt, this book would not have come into being. I would also like to thank my beloved Maria for writing, reading, and listening to poetry with me and continuing to inspire me with the brightness she brings into the world.

-PEFB

CONTENTS

The Hummingbird / 1

University / 3

Define Me / 6

Beauty's Quiddity / 9

Epistemic Piecemeal / 11

Another Day at School / 13

The Capitalist Conqueror / 15

Picking Words / 17

The Eight Beer Hammer / 19

Matter's Motives / 21

A Walk in the Park / 22

In The Air / 23

Looking up / 24

Whirled Rulers / 25

A Limerick / 29

A Goodbye / 30

A Haiku or Two / 31

For Ruedi and Whitney's Wedding / 32

For the Homeless man on Father's Day / 33

The Cold Outside / 35

After the Fourth Season / 36

Rubik's Cube / 37

The Disconnect / 38

On Why to Avoid a Gold Rush / or Emptiness / 40

The Text Song of Timothy M. Prufrock / 42

Carryout Pizza Poem / 48

In search of Mexican Food / 49

From the Bosom of the Abyss / 50

Coffee Date / 53

Between the Digeridoos and the Digeridon'ts / 55

For Robert / 57

With Open Hands / 60

WWI: Can War be Great? / 62

Stockholm Syndrome of the Superego / 65

Divvying up the Divine / 69

Blue / 72

Macy's Postmodern Goose / 74

The Smell of History / 77

Dasein / 79

Who is my Brother? / 81

With which of the Fives Senses do You Feel
   Belonging? / 84

Voiceless / 88

For my dad, Randall Scott Frost, whose music and memory still bring brightness to the world.

The Hummingbird

I.
Lifeless and lonely, the mahogany body
rests in the corner.
The strings stretched across rosewood—
as silent as sunset—
shimmering in the dim light,
as I walk by remembering
the hands that moved
the strings to sing
and lifted me
up to your shoulder.
The melodies you made
by strumming steel,
which vibrated and fluttered—
and softly set that sweet
sound in my ear,
now sleep with you.
The black hole stares at me
from its hollow wood
haunting me with the emptiness
of the silence with you not here.

II.
When I strum
to make the bird hum
I'm holding your hand
as I retrace your fingerprints
on the rosewood fingerboard.
Finger picking incites the echo
of fading memories
with your singing smile
and warm hands dancing upon
the piano keys and your fingers
freely frolicking
among the frets.
You sang with all your soul
about hope and life for the lost.
That warmth reverberates still
in the tone emanating
from her aging wood,
but I play a sadder sound—
of solemn songs
in a minor key—
as if it were a dirge—
or *goodbye dad*
that I had no way to say
when I was seven.

University
(Like my education, this poem is in progress)

Far too often i am much too like J. Alfred Prufrock.
As I sit to think, the questions
upon my head begin to knock;
but how shall I answer?
This I cannot tell, at least not well,
for clarity is obscured from me.
While I sit awake, many directions
I might take; but while I am dreaming
they all come streaming
mounting back to my indecision;
and what shall I do?
Write a paper? Take a test?
I will strive for excellence
in ultimate frisbee
and lose rest studying.

The questions are pressing
I cannot stop guessing
what is it that I am for?
I should have been a knob upon a door
that I might have brought closure.

As I pass through the doors
of the educational edifice,
I find certainty in the wealth of knowledge.
The glistening gold of social science

Grant explanations of humankind
the dazzling diamonds
of scientific determinacy
delineate (define away the doubts)
of mysterious causation,

bricks of empirical observations
mortared together constructing
the edifice of knowledge
housing uncertain certainties
constructed on skeptical doubt.

Professors professing moral messages of freedom:
Let your wild oats flow free,
but only as free as water is free to fall.1
Books bashing the bastions
of ancient outdated ideals.

In the past few centuries
the age of science has made its entrance
among the dead manatees
what a glorious new appliance
will cook my dinner.
I have yet to see solution
to the perpetually pressing questions
I have yet to see science make humans humane
or inter the deceitful inhibition of avarice
to progressive progression
but from my digression I regress to the questions:
what are we for?

Fit my mind inside your Newtonian World Machine
axiomatic methods axing at my volition.
If you put the universe into a bottle,
and manipulated it as you do throttle,
you could tell me how it twirls and loops, loops and swirls,
of the nexus of necessary causal connections
declare why the system persists,
but you have failed to explain
why in the first it exists.
With all the talking and models of the past
you cannot see at last
that your solutions are reduced to poetry2.

1. See Hobbes *Leviathon*
2. Albert Camus, *The Myth of Sisyphus*

Define Me

Define me,
hold the totality of my existence in your gaze,
and in a phrase be certain that you know me.
Hang me on a category
rigidly designate my worth
by the location of my birth.
Catch sight of my tattered brown shoes
and confine me in a word:
unforgivable

Define me,
by how fast I go when the light turns green,
but my face grows red by your defining
your rigid designations I am defying.
Let your impatience be your guide,
cut me off, for I slowly drive.
Hit me with your condescending gaze,
fuming, leave me in the haze of your exhaust.
Surely you know why

Define me with a glance,
my whole mental framework,
by a single political stance.
By a single green bumper sticker,
lump me in *The Left* of liberal losers.
From a red campaign sticker with a name,
you can name all my qualities:

asinine, arrogant, capitalist, patriotic.
Might I myself exist apart from vitriolic bicker
of dichotomous definitions of political positions.

By the shaggy hair I wear and the rusted car I drive,
surely you know why I strive to be alive.
By the callous on my hand:
my social class you understand,
and my ill-mannered life you reprimand.

You have defined me.
By the size of my waist:
you know whether I deserve praise
and the measure of my days.
Oh, but I waste away in your words.

But might not the line circumscribing me
be more blurred?
And from something other born?
A few conversations and you categorize me by my
likeness to others.
But can't you see this smothers the me in me?
Hire me in thirty-five minutes
for you know if I'll be productive for you.
In a glance or a handshake, whether I can be friends
with you.

Indeterminate, I might exist,
between the lines of your specific definitions.
Beyond the white picket fence of your first impressions

But from fencing me in and cutting me off,
the sum of my existence lunges toward autonomous being
attempting to skillfully foil your cutting summations.

Let my soul be savage before it is fettered by your endless definitions.
I will revolt against your knowing by my ominous premonitions.

Beauty's Quiddity

Beauty ephemerally danced,
as I stood entranced by her captivating glow,
but in that moment I reached out to grasp,
yet she passed through my hand like a sound.
What about her so resounds in my soul?

In a voluminous rock stretched out against the sky,
beauty mysteriously succeeded in lifting my soul.
She, in the mountain's granite, granted me pleasure.
When the sun slid beyond my sight,
in the color that burned upon the clouds,
her symphony echoed loudly through my core.

Beauty flew through threw the window
carried on the wings of sound.
Feathering my heart with her arrows,
impelling me into the hall.
As I passed through the door,
the harmonious melody
floating from the guitar moved me.
How could vibrations from skillfully plucked strings
ring in my being with such awful wonder?

I have caught evanescent glimpses of her
like lightning flashing behind, illuminating everything
before me, but when I turn round
I fail to find the electrifying splendor in my sight.

I spotted her on the rolling waves,
and in the silver glaze on the crystal lake
beneath the gentle breeze and soothing moon.

I sought to find her, to define her,
I think I might have actually seen her face.
In trying to fix her being in my mind's eye
she dissipated into the distant corners of the universe.
With jubilation and mystification, she filled me.
I wondered why, when she walked by,
and she put my heart into a whirlwind.
I thought I knew; I ran to catch her pulchritude,
and facetiously, she floated upon the breeze into the bushes.
Her cogent quiddity eluded me still.

Epistemic Piecemeal

Thoughts flow—
disconnected like molecules:
words swirling around ideas-
separated by space
connected by intangible forces,
holding my perspective
and the world in place.

Sounds carrying
convoluted connotations—
fractured images conveyed
through differing intonations—
refurbishing beliefs like
plaid vinyl couches.

Concepts congealing into red Picasso
-esque melodramas called memories
faces fragmented and twisted into ideas
beliefs relieving
surreptitious sailors of fearful
reservations about unending sailing—
claiming *Land Ho, this I know*.

motivations meander
through forests of neural pathways
from tree to tree the axon-winds
carrying intentions of actions—waving
fragmented perceptions *frantically* bow hunting cohesion.

Chaos augmented by GREEN—*dog's barks;* wind waving
my hair & recollection of a thousand memories of
moments=with Elmer's GLUED into the instant of
NOW.

I am becoming a necromancer
of interred mythologies—
piecemealing philosophic pancakes
together with Aunt Jemima Syrup—
bringing forth buried beliefs
to uphold precarious conventions.
Dead dogmas barking with absolutes

webs of perceptions tangled clearly in my nest- hidden
alone in the
corner— the act I've known as
Knowing

Another Day at School

The frozen smoking car explodes with potential
stilled and silent in a flash—
frozen in a photo.
                After the fourth grade class from across
                                the street
            had come outside to study ecosystems—
                  the foundations of life:
        darting birds crunching grasshoppers
              who were eating grass
the red hatted man in his black yellow banded uniform
runs toward the thick smell of burning rubber—
and burning flesh,
carrying a black snake that breaths death to fire
and life to survivors—
a picture of heroism.
            Lebanese politics produce unfortunate
                  side effects.
The dynamite of political praxis detonated
a Toyota with the potential of policymaking.
            Before the class syllabus for the day changed:
              to study human nature: beneficent/degraded,
                  to study physics: causes and effects;
                          and
                to observe the fireworks of dissidence
                    and to see nine people

spread in pieces across the parking lot
creating crimson pools of political capital
as if to confirm when Aristotle said
Political Science is the greatest-
end of man.

The Capitalist Conqueror

As his wing-tips whet the sidewalk
with want of swallowing,
the high rises look down
and despise his impudence.
Through his redolent cologne,
the smog coughs at his pretension;
the passing cars sneer
at his ostentatious look.
A black Beemer angrily swerves
to splash sludge on his gaudy suit;
even his Rolex rolls its eyes
at his arrogant brows.

He sits as king of the hill
singing his overcoming praise.
CEO of the corporate world:
self-declared thus for all his days.

Climbing on bloody knees and elbows,
laboring long into the nights,
and lingering long after the commuters came
from suburbs: morning after morning.
His ingenuity and strength paving
the way for cajoling the acquiescent
consenters to take roles in his pernicious plan.
Clerks, techies, secretaries, and accountants
becoming pawns and cogs; lives contorting
to the monetary machination of his insular caprice.

After bowing before the Bottom Line,
he ascended the ladder by clawing
the flesh from the backs of the lazy.
Running towards deadlines, he stomped
the heads of the disadvantaged: crushing ears,
loosening teeth, wetting eyes with blood and tears.

Beggars can't be choosers.

Convalescence

Passing the park, he caught a glance
of the pigeons laughing at his lost luxury.

Picking Words

Words, I think, can be not somewhat unlike
a rented 75 cent arm
which might pick out
a coveted Stretch Armstrong,
or a spotted stuffed cow,
but the cold metal claw will usually
come up empty.
Words might also reach
for the Barry Bonds doll,
but instead grabbing
the undesirable rainbow-haired Troll baby
compatible only with bb gun target practice.
Words, however, might also pick a stuffed bear
by lifting the bear from its buried den
beneath the cow and Armstrong
with gangly fingers clasping the bear—
the indexical arm of reference swaying—
almost crushing the soft and huggable meaning
before
awkwardly
      dropping
           the
                toy
                    into the prize bin—of your ear.
                    So I am sorry that I have not
                    yet mastered this rented 75
                    cent arm. I apologize that while

attempting to grab that
snuggly bear for you, you instead
received a squeaky dog toy.
For this, and all my other
misappropriated
meanings, I am sorry.

The Eight Beer Hammer

Our tree got in a car accident
with a drunk man last night.
That veritable protector from sun and storm
stepped in to stop
that spinning, sliding sledge hammer of Izuzu.
My sister thought the fridge fell over
at the quaking of our house
at the cracking of our tree.
It was eight or nine beers, he said,
that hammered our tree.
The silver speeder skipped the curb,
skated across snow
covered grass before
embracing the beech.
The car laid there
like a beached whale—smoking,
it's rear bumper slightly
bending our mailbox.
Broken branches and bumper
shattered and scattered
for one hundred feet in all directions.
Her hood and six cylinders forming a C
where she had once encircled our tree.
Thirty-two years of shade,
spring, and fall—broken.

The cold winter's night now drunken
with his sap, split in two,
dying as the frigid air
froze away his base.
He saved us, from a drunk man
and his car, last night.

Matter's Motives

Is it for love or money
that atoms make molecules?
Was it fate that brought
2H and O together
into such blessed harmony
that this rock is a habitable home?
Or by choice
that carbon combines into
components that make life?
Was it neurochemistry
that made hydrogen so unstable
that he caught the Hindenberg
in such a great conflagration?
Is it for Helen
that war still blazes
in the burning of the sun?
Was it necessity
that caused the ecstasy
of endorphins to exult my heart
at the sight of you?
Was it upbringing
or endowment
that so pissed off Uranium
that he threw his decay
on everyone?
Oh Hiroshima! Oh Nagasaki!
How your molecules bled and burned—
So many dear bonds broken
The unleashed power of the atom
has changed everything.

A Walk in the Park

    I remember when—
           when we were friends
    then the sun set
           when I turned your shoulders cold
    ending footsteps from the park

    snow fills the air with the silence
           of your words, with the slicing
    of your avoidant eyes, eying corners
           my foot, and heart, sinking in
                        the snow—
                    alone
    without the sunshine and laughter
           of your rising smile

    laughing as we walked,
           I tripped you—bruising your heart

In the Air

It's a lot like falling in love
when accelerating,
the paved path runs away.
Moving far above
where cement swallows
moribund meadows.
What is this petulant turbulence
between my ribs?
Lofted above the morass
of Mondays and deadlines,
that died from the doom of boredom.
It happened one night—
the whirling turbines pulling me
to the back of my seat,
dancing flaps and ailerons
directing—
butterflies dancing and flapping
toward my esophagus,
taking my voice.
Excited high into the open sky-blue
at the thought of you leaving,
the wings disintegrating.
Propelled onward, flying forward, thrust upward,
wobbling in the uncertain wind:
steadied with you in view.
By the loveliness of your eyes in my gaze
I am grounded.

Looking Up

Night falls—
like heads from the guillotine.
Parades of sorrow
dance in the streets of thought
for the revolution.
Mutinous motivation forsakes my crown
to reside in my foot soles, inept.
The pernicious peasantry
of failed intentions advancing.
Tears tearing down the Bastille,
causing the kingdom of me
to collapse upon the floor.
The Château de Sense
set on fire, torn down,
by serfs of sadness.

The fair face of hope fell
beheaded,
her rolling head ended—
                              looking up.

Whirled Rulers

Someone must rule—
be it the toddler in his drool
or the fool in his fun;
maybe the son of privilege feeding
the world his silver spoon
ideologies of revolution,
or the ogre in his drivel
yet the school girls will still giggle
at the boys who employ
awkward words to demonstrate
ploys for dominance.
King of the hill will still
govern earth's playgrounds in determining
the strongest, and excluding the lame
and the weak and the meek
from the throne,
but who shall inherit the earth
upon its rebirth?
Will chattering opinions
take dominion of this whirled
rock inhabited by upright walking
crooked talking humanoids?
Who, taken together, are devoid
of the sense called common and waver
like leaves in the wind,
quaking with fright at the might
of the Unknown.

Yet science, (we hope) will
soon explain her out of doubt
with hypotheses, diagrams, and charts
to define away
the unknowable
so we can pretend to plan
with certainty.
Someone must lead
through the weeds of unfruitful
ideas. Ideally, one who knows
the thoughts that won't miscarry
and make us bury another generation
of our world's young boys
who died for fascism and freedom
and other fantastic political fantasies
that resulted in this apoplectic society.
But who will doctor us back to right?
From the wrongs that turn the world around
at our corporate inhumanity
with the dignity we lack to see
in the eyes, looking into the hearts,
of others: our human sisters
and brothers. Who, equally positioned
in this unchangeable condition of servitude,
hope for serenity.
We could always let me rule.
Not I, myself, of course.
But the conglomerate "I"
that vast appetite that has
the "I"s to see our own advantage

individually. In our egalitarian equality,
equal each in our own desire to
consume the world
wearing stilettos
and talking of power politics.
Desiring sameness.
Equality that will eat all distinctions
and erase the troublesome differences
of class and those amassed at the line
of gender. We have a right to work
to equal pay, to have our say in all
we do or do not do. You can't tell me
I'm wrong, because I can know as well as you
and I read it in the paper. I can
snooze through life reading my e-news
of emu societal relations.

Corporations have volunteered
to lead the world with greed
turning tides and rolling nations
under a green banner
governed by one absolute—
the truth of which cannot be questioned:
shareholders must receive a profit
no matter what the cost
in oily tides or loss of lives.
They will strip the earth bare,
the little child's finger bare
so you can wear a sweat-shopped
sweatshirt, and bear the banner

of corporate branding to impress
friends with how much you spent
but they don't care, unless
they have invested in
that corporate person's icon.
You don't need a priest
or steeple to worship now.
You may bow before your
clear picture of your idols
on your LCD TV
and in adulation
buy what they tell you
you need.
In the free world,
the middle class and up
is chained in stocks
and bonds
the lower class gave up
ladder climbing:
position locked
and wounded.

A Limerick

For topics disjointed and dismal
I recommend pseudo-Pepto-Bismol
cure intellectual indigestion
of the boring blunt bastion
before sordid lines vomit abysmal

A Goodbye at a Friend's Wedding

Time will do
to do or undo
the meaning of me and you
friendships, like other aging ships,
can sink
or be refurbished
to sail on other seas

A Haiku or Two

When dying leaves fall
turn to dust beneath the sky
naked trees ask why

trees color the sky
leaves dance a wind blown romance
Winter falls towards love

For Ruedi and Whitney's Wedding

Love
grows with
time—through breaks & rain,
from joy and pain it blooms,
with sunshine.
Smiles uniting
with a kiss,
lives colliding
taking off
into bliss.
A boy and a girl
striking notes
blossoming
into harmony.

For the Homeless Man on Father's Day

Beneath a faded, torn ball cap
lies a bearded face with forlorn eyes
and a mouth with cracked lips
that would open
to tell me a story
if I asked—
But I was too busy...
busy working to
avoid his eyes
that might upset
my complacency.
To avoid his
reading questions
with their hands
stretching for
my pockets and hard earned
or rather, easily borrowed green.
It was his bag that
brought out my aversion.
The green frayed
canvas burden,
that carried everything—
all of his possessions:
his sleeping bag and stories.
Yet it is too small
to carry his now weary dreams
of smiling children
who might have run to him

yelling *papa papa,*
or a bed of his own
those dreams,
like the ball cap he wears,
have faded
traded for the heavy
weight he carries
on his back.
The drill sergeant
called him degenerate
the psychologist found
him to be an aberration
his boss
told him he was distracted
and he contracted
a melancholic disposition
and wandered   off

The Cold Outside

The flip-flops
and song birds of spring
with blossoming daffodils
and blossoming love
have become long lonely nights.
wintery cold has
hardened the honey
in the cupboards.
my hand
had been enchanted
by a more delicate
touch, but now holds
this tea cup—
un-warmed.
Sorrow drips
into the melting
puddles of snow,
with nowhere to flow
until spring.

After the Fourth Season

The cacophony of crickets, cooing doves,
and copulating crows
inters the winter's dreary peace.
The white painted perfection of snow
is dissolved and swallowed
by the harsh sun.
The enchantment of Apollo
draws out the daffodils.
When the ants come marching,
who is April fooling—
but the apparent, near pandemic
death in foliage?
The pines persisted alone in their defiance
waving the green flag of life
in the dead of winter.
The spiral-wound coils contained in trees
spring and unwind, unfurling leaves
leaving the grim reaper's season destitute.
How does it feel when death dies
beneath the rainy sky
and the spritely chaos
of the world made new?

Rubik's Cube

Life is a game of twists and turns
and color sequences
filled with far too many squares.
It is a child's simple matching task
of mind bending confusion.
Algorithms provide solace
for rule following problem-solvers
but what creative fire is there
in someone else's formula?
Ought we prefer uniformity
to a confused and colorful
attempt at personal attainment?
Life I'm afraid has more than six colors
and is more than a three-axis event.
There is also no world-record
for solving it blindfolded.
I have not solved it yet
but I will keep twisting
perplexed, as I strive
for harmony and balance.

The Disconnect

Unlike the noiseless spider,
I am not patient
my gossamer threads keep reaching, overreaching
and never landing

I can feel my soul shriveling—
the panic of directionless passion,
shallow breaths,
despair descends in the cellar of my spirit
in an attempt to barricade from the tornado
of tormenting absurdity

Happiness has become a dusty fiction—
a faded memory I read of decades ago
the white picket fence of myself that I presented
now swirls skyward
my hidden hopes and quiet ideals are exposed
as the storm steals the roof from over the attic,
wet and darkened by the disjointing fingers of despair.
My I-beams bending from the assault:
my mental framework of assumed certainties
crushed beneath the weight
of the lofted limbs of neighboring trees
power lines likewise severed:
I am powerless— unable to move.
Phone lines and feelings disconnected
the outage makes for no outgoing calls.

In the cellar, water rises as the foundation weakens.
I am become apathy: destroyer of empires.

My failures, my faults,
my thousand indecisions
and bad decisions
are the hail that shatters
and have uncovered me.
Are the wind that dissects me
I am undone by the weight of my doubt.
Guilt is the branch that has crushed
all that I thought I was or could be.
Shame has cut off the phones and power
paralyzing my volition completely.

What of the splintering beams on Calvary?
Did He take my shame and guilt?
Will I fall on that Rock and be broken
or try to repair the breaches
limping in isolation?

On Why to Avoid a Gold Rush / or Emptiness

I went out in search
of your beauty
with our hands clasped together
as we walked beneath
warmth of the summer sun
in mountain meadows.
I became a miner
determined to unearth the diamonds
concealed beneath your faux faces.
Armed only with a pick axe of petunias
a shovel of sunflowers and warm words
and geologic amounts of time

Many times the moon waxed and then melted away
until again the leaves abandoned their places.
Before a panorama of snowy peaks
I panned for gold,
hoping to find in that frigid stream
at least a speck
of sunshine to lead me
to the light for my soul
that was promised
by the twinkle in your eye
and lightness of your laughter

For seven years
with leathery hands and empty eyes
through blizzards and your icy stares
I kept holding on and digging deeper
often wearily collapsing
under the weight of your disdain
digging past your stone-faced affection
with shovel in hand and my brows furrowed
only to exhume the frostbitten and gaunt
corpse of my own soul.
The only diamond I found
was to know the truth
that it was I
who had been empty—all along
the glisten of life in your eyes
and all of the warmth
of your kindnesses was not enough
to keep the biting winter wind at bay
and instead of gold or diamonds
all I found in you
was the sharp dark pain
of haunting isolation
that I had run so long from
in the vast cavern
of my heart

The Text Song of Timothy M. Prufrock
For my grandfather, J. Alfred, the better lover.

I'm sorry you
didn't get a text right back
from me.
I was temporally distracted
by the clicking clock hands
pointing their fingers
at the gap between
the funny guy
you thought I was
two texts ago
and the disappointment
you will find
in twenty texts
or twenty years.

Turning my back on you
and walking away
right in the middle
of our lengthy conversation
about politics and
the theory of friendship
was not what I meant to do,
but my roommate put on
an explosive action flick
and you in my phone, got left
on the kitchen table.

No I was not trying
to pay you back
for all the times you left me
hanging
in a noose of expectation
threaded by all the emojis
and coy banter
which created in my mind
the image of the likeness of
an emotional connection
built up to that precipice
with that winky face emoji
that made me think that
maybe you were feeling
just what I was feeling.
As my heart rate increased
with the wonder that you might express…
—Then silence—

Around the town,
the women walk and frown
looking down
eyes fixed on phone screens

Text-response, text-response
we proceeded at a nearly automated pace
as I poured my soul
into letters that lost
that feeling through the transmission towers
and ones and zeros

spilling into your phone
as silent black and white text and
an occasional cartoon expression
in an attempt to re-humanize myself.
At my joke you purported
to laugh out loud, but
I knew better—
I at least imagined
a smile appearing
lifting the edges of your distant eyes.

I grow bored, I grow bored

when you speak through SMS
I imagine you with a
breastplate like Athena
as your hair flutters in the breeze
kissed with the golden touch of the sun
your words roll forth
in buttery smoothness
until I h-e-r-e r-o-n-g
*correction H-e-a-r w-r-o-n-g
grammatical failings
harpooning me back
to see that all I know of you is text.

So I wonder
do I dare and
do you care?

In a minute there is time
for mistelling and misspelling
which a later minute cannot reverse.

Do I dare disturb—
the server
about the question
that was dropped
upon my plate?
Or to say I said
hold the artichokes.
But when I am hanging there
in the thread of your non-responses
and the weight
if your disdaining glances
how shall I begin
to cough out
those three words
To keep you
from walking away?

I should have been an ant
shuffling on jungle floors
that I might not walk alone.

When I look
to look into your eyes
I only see the glinted smudged reflection
of my own in my smartphone.

That's not what I meant
to spell
that's not what I meant at all.

When we met for coffee
your words came out
like collapsing blocks at the end of JENGA

I understand why
you didn't look at me
while we ate.
How could I compete
with a retweet from Kimye?
At me, you only rolled your eyes
never on the floor with laughter.
My attempts at clever word play
fall flat beneath the hilarity
of an angry cat.
The whole world
is at your fingertips
while an entire world away
I anxiously age—
across the table.
What could I say
to keep your interest?
When your friends
keep pinning recipes—
for happiness.
Why would you choose
to turn your eyes toward me when

There is that young goose Ryan
longingly looking at you
with a suave *hey girl.*
With all its unreliability
that Wiki still has a better
memory than me.
And you remember
all my forgettings.

I cannot look in the mirror
without the fear
that the chime of one of your arriving
texts is that time,
the terminal tock of the clock for us.
You ex-ing me out to be —Oh— so alone.
for my apostate punctuality and abundant frugality

No, I am no Steve Rogers
nor was meant to be.
Am merely supporting cast
one to pass a line or two
and run at the sight of danger.
They will say, they will say:
my how his beard is thin
my how his hair thins
but oh, his portfolio is thinner.
Do I dare disturb the Universe?
Like my hairline,
I keep retreating from those whom I face.

Carryout Pizza Poem

Have you ever seen the sunshine
in the middle of the blackest storm?
when the sky splits in two
and through the sheets of water
you look straight
into the luminescence of life itself?
I watched the trees clap their hands
and fall prostrate
before that power
the roads were replaced with rivers
on Metcalf Ave the transformer
was transformed
into a violent fireball fountain of light
lightening the night with severity.
Night became day in the pulsating shocks.
The city went dark—
the only thing between me and melting
from its electricity
was wet splashing circuitry.
I imagined the darkening
of the spark of my own heart
wondering
what song might sound
on the other side of the thunder,
and whether
the late night run was worth it
for the spice
of jalapeno pepper pizza?

In Search of Mexican Food

In a twist of fate or irony,
the ungroomed benevolent bovine
groomed the green growing ground
because he cud
well, could, but cud would naturally follow.
Ruminating on the rolling hills
and the gastronomic intricacies
of highland leafy luxury.
With that manner of manor
and that fur that fluffs
how could he not be the envy
of all oxen this side of Urals?
A passing cloud caught his gaze
as if a wisp of a mirror—
he saw his own fluffiness floating by:
thoughts drifting onward
not of nirvana, but reincarnation,
life hereafter
as a fluffy foot rug
and as a savory stew,
but not as carne asada.

From the Bosom of the Abyss

I'm looking into it,
said the soon curiously killed cat.
Nine lives or not there is no protection
when the Abyss stares back into you.
All the punctuated pleasantries of
everyday unawareness
with their autos, and ads, and coffee cups
finally add up—to less than nothing.
Everyday aspirations for comfort and connection
disintegrate into the spinning perspiration
of gerbil wheels as the distance between us
multiplies with every step toward you as Zeno's
Paradox of the Illusion of Movement
makes every gap an infinitely un-crossable gulf.

Why do I keep crawling back to the darkness?
Where nuzzling into its bosom gives no warmth
but like an arid wicked winter night
it pulls the warmth from your skin
so you don't realize you are cold
until there is only frigid biting pain remaining.

Why do I wrap myself in a blanket of despair?
Maybe I return because in that barren barrage
of powerlessness
I feel the familiar fire of an empty hearth
and it smells more like home
than any other scent on this earth.

Feeling that the most honest mirror I have met
was my darkened reflection
in the deafening silence of nothingness.
In the deepest most protected part of my heart
lies
a languishing sense of lack
and like a mother cat she grabs me by the scruff
and from my anguish I respond with placidity
and paralysis
in buried memory of her
non-nurturing in infancy
leading me to the conclusion,
as I lie curled up-on the floor,
that I had when I began: I am not enough.
I
am
lack

Lies—
not easily undone
by makeshift mantras
or the power of positive thinking
that keep no charge in the vast swallowing
engine of entropy
can ontology be undone by anything but doing?
I know not how many lives I have left,
but I'd rather spend this one in the warmth of the sun
delighting in the summer cicada-ian rhythms
and the delicate dance of daffodils.
Finding freedom in friendship that dissolves
the sense of absolute isolation

in the interconnectedness of being-together
where my thoughts are
in the mirror of the other
illuminated by the light of love.
Abba abate my blindness
let the hearth of my heart
burn with the fire of your feeling
wrap me in a blanket of belonging
that I might find the warmth of being
in bringing light into the world.
Plug my ears
to the sirens' song of sadness
that I would instead find sweetness
in giving kindness
let me feel the sunshine of your gaze
in your image in the face
of the person in front of me
that there might be green growing
in the garden of my soul.
That in the tumult of the world's turning tides
I might have belonging in a home
to return to inside
that in the wonder of your words
I would smell the sweetness of home.
Let the vast expanse of emptiness
carved out in my heart
become a cistern of compassion
for the broken
that in the spilling over of that rising well
I would find life.

Coffee Date

Is there enough overlap
in our mental maps
to chart a future—together?
Does our metaphysical topography agree?
With lines drawn in the right places
indicating a parallel
hierarchy of spaces:
rises and falls of rights and wrongs?
Does our moral cartography comport?
Or is there an intolerable variance
in our values of kindness?
Could there be enough flexibility
in the map
to find forgiveness when it bends
the wrong way
and to not rip in the rain?
Is there enough harmony in our views
of the destiny of reality
that we could camp out
with good intent
on the same realty?

I want to become a student
of your pupils
that they might enlighten me
with their alluring illumination
such depth and vivacity

might have the capacity
to fill the sail of my soul,
but for how long?
Might my grandchildren
brighten the world
with the warmth
of your smile?
I guess to see
I'll have to start by
summoning the courage
to form the words
with my mouth:
would you—like
to get coffee,
no, scratch that—
would you like to go out
for pasta
with   me?

Between the Digeridoos and the Digerdon'ts

lies the original aboriginal
mixolydian melody of ambivalence
dissonant harmonies melodicizing
the metaphysical montage
of the surreal soundscapes we inhabit
decibels demur the silence
slicing it into aural delicacies.
Deontological truths trumpet
clearly murky certainties into classical
symphonic soliloquys,
while John Stuart Mills
must have meant pop music
when he spoke of the greatest good
for the greatest number
one hits, humdrum utilitarian ukulele
loiters with the tired tunes of campfire carols.

It sounds good to me she said,
mistaking the truncated
triplets of traffic tumult
for the distant hum
of the music of spheres.
Never has cocaine sounded as good
as when the Bird brought forth
dancing bebop butterflies
to jazz up the clubs.

The last straw of Stravinsky
was broken
when tonality tuned out
at Derrida's dubstep
deconstruction dance:
the jackhammer jig

For Robert

Tears transmogriphy
terrestrial terraces
into abstract
unknown spaces
tearing down
any semblance
of sensibility
until I cannot recognize
the ground beneath my feet
grief governs grimly—
how the world moves
in the center
of a landslide of loss
and what can I hold on to
when there is no bottom
to the falling
and flailing
my upward reach
spins downward?
North in not to be found
when my internal
compass corrodes
at the crack in reality
realizing that
at the Cafe
you will never again
serve up your soft-spoken kindness.

The Mercer lines of my mental map
collapse into Spiraling parabolas.
Did you ever enjoy the cigar I got you
for your birthday?
Before the bacteria,
the hospital bed,
your intubated wordless breaths—
I saw kindness and hope still in your eyes
as I prayed, then said goodbye
I drove back to Missouri
you lay in Colorado
and then took that terminal trip
I didn't drive back
to say goodbye again
to your then breathless body
not knowing
the last words I heard from you.

Has your jeep journeyed
without you
rolling over mountain rocks
to Golden aspen views?
Does your Rottweiler
still semi-regularly rip up
trespassing skunks?
And watch the door
waiting for you
to come home?
The world keeps spinning
in its typical insanity

and I hold on to the thought
of your smile
as you rocket forward
on your electric assist bike
in the world to come.

With Open Hands

Happiness is not a big enough word
to contain an answer
to the question mark
my heart has etched
into the fabric
of my own being
the many orisons
my horizon has housed
face off against the waves
of unknowing
that break against my back
when I try to hold on
to a singular overly small
tale of the true.

Possibility cannot be held
with a closed hand.
I can make no certain
demands of the unfolding.

What deeper hues
will future heartbreaks hone
to see brighter
the brilliant budding
in the following year's
fruitful fields?

Is the sharp pain
in reality's constant change
really surprising?
When our first launch into life
is a screaming entrance
into exile
from the constant warmth
of the womb?

We, journeying now as refugees
in our own isolation,
hope to find that
sense of connection again—
that somewhere
was made for us.

Made now
in wisdom and words
with rituals and kindnesses
a fabric knit together
of our and others' intentions
bigger than the crippling confines
of my own head.
A way toward becoming.

WWI: Can War be Great?

Mordor was a real place
in France during the so called *Great War*
hellfire and brimstone hailed down
rearranging the idyllic pastureland
Into lifeless lunar landscapes
flaming still as
crimson waves of men
charged forward
and in the pastures
were mowed down like hay
with tommy guns, grenades, and shells.
Raining: oceans of shells—exploding
rural wineries ran red with life of Frenchman
mustard gas pollinated champagne
vines with poison.

Men burrowed like naked mole rats into the earth
—exposed
hiding their blind eyes from the red cloud of death
drifting across no man's land
while drifting in and out
of their own humanity
waiting for the sky to fall
in flashes and explosions.

Bullets for deserters
or the brave patriots

fighting for God and country
ending entrenched
between this world and the next.

As austere men in mustaches
meandered through elegant hallways,
sat upon ancient upholstered chairs
concerning themselves with maps
and the finer points
of international treaties and the theories of war
postulating precise patterns to obtain victory
as Caesar's crossing of the Rhine
or Alexander annexing the world by bravery
chivalry and love of the fatherland or motherland
must not be diminished.
No sacrifice could be too great
to preserve their pride.
Czar-Kaiser-King crowned by God
embodying country
and demanding human sacrifices
more gruesome
than Aztecs eating beating hearts.

In the remaining rubble of Europe
only a heap of shattered souls remain.

The industrial age accelerated
to advance the potentialities of humankind.
To manufacture automobiles
and extract oil

and create instruments of destruction
unimaginable by the science fiction
of the generation before

the shrapnel lodged in the continent's
collective soul
and festered fastidiously
beneath the surface of perception
birthing a war
—greater—
in destruction

Stockholm Syndrome of the Superego

When I went out
in search
of myself
I didn't expect to find
myself
a stranger
in the yet still
stranger land
where I began

I spoke with Seneca
about Senates and empires
and slaves
and surrender
to the emperor
and
the profound isolation
of considering what
contests will come
in the coliseum
of myself
the emperor, my superego,
with a stoic gaze
and a statuesque face
and a fastidious grasp on the good
and the right
hand fixed

with an extended thumb
in a downward direction
denoting death
to my imprisoned passions
pinned down at the spears end
of my self-loathing
the enamoring sound
of my self-critique
and it's narrow views

Man of God
there is death
in the pot
of the stew
in my head
and Elisha said
add a handful
of salt

Sodium chloride
breaks into sodium ions
which break into neurons
which break into these broken thoughts

Wondering how to effectuate
action potentials in axons
is ineffective as a means of achieving anything
other than thought about thought.
Thoughts extending further and further
over the unthinkable gulf

between self and brain,
until the positive potassium ions
are charged off.
I can only outwit myself
when my ego and id,
at the direction of the super,
take a vacation together
in the less than balmy
clime of despair.
My attempts at introspection
interweaving together
into tightly wound webs of inaction

So wise it sounds
speaking softly,
my own voice,
in the back of my head
whispering images
of taut truths
tying me in knots of trepidation
of the negativities portended
by any possibility
and praising the pause of passivity

Reaching high will only bring failure
a higher climb will only mean a further fall

A waking trance tips me into a tumble
hearing the voice
of the five-year-old tyrant's tantrum

his staunch stories
losing plausibility as I see him
from behind the curtain
sliding lugubrious levers
with his bottom lip upturned.
So much less enchanting
than I had thought

There are more things ... likely to frighten us than there are to crush us; we suffer more often in imagination than in reality. Seneca

Divvying up the Divine

What wonder wastes away
beneath the collapsing corpses of cathedrals
as August arches atrophy
colored windows once steered our thoughts
towards stories of sacrifice and magnanimity
celestial ceilings soared high to lift
our eyes and minds to remember
there is something above us.
The stars sang together emanating ethereal radiance
the night sky, which rang with unknown wonder
with innumerable heavenly lights,
now drones on
with the distant burning of gases
each with a distance and mass.
The stars have greater mass than the Catholics now—
even if they might have burned out
before the birth of the dearth of humane society.

La Luna,
the lady of the night,
shares her soft luminescence
and conducts the tides
in a cyclical symphony.
Now she wanes
trodden underfoot
by one small step of man.
Her warmth and wonder
replaced by barren dust and rocks
bagged up by a lunar rover.

Our spires are now crowned with the hum
of florescent lights split up in cubes
with desks
to further divide us
to pursue
the possibility
money brings
our thoughts
now lifted upward
by printed paper
portraits
on the cover of Forbes
chasing mirages
of our own grandeur
the lofty elevation
of the value
in our accounts.

Breathe
spirit
suspire.

What are we
but water and fire
and earth enlivened
by breath?
Breathe in the wonder of being
the wonder of being matter that thinks itself
the matter of wonder washes over our being
in this quixotic quest to continue breathing
bringing back the mystery—

the vast expanse beyond our grasp
wherein divinity dreams—
decrying denotation—
the inimitable ineffable aura
awakens aspirations
to reach again
upward
toward
the divine
giver of breath

Blue

When the bat sends sounds skyward
what does it see?
Does the vast expanse of emptiness
above *feel* blue?
What keeps the blind leather birds
from flying high above
the bugs' abodes?
Can they hear the songs
of the stars, the ether?

When I look into the stretched out splashing surf
above the plunging depths
that swallow all soundings,
how does it compare to when
I look into the astoundingly vast
(3/4 inch) depth in my own blue eyes?

If blue had a texture,
I think it would be smooth,
not like velvet.
More like the viscosity of a milkshake
cold and thick, though less refreshing.
Like the feeling of staring into the darkness
of an empty ceiling
unmovable, alone.

My thought of blueness (a theory of blue)
rests securely somewhere in a blue
floating chair upon which I sit
in the air— suspended
between the ceiling and a child
crying next to me giving me
a feeling of

                        weight
                             ed-
                                n
                                e
                                s
                                s

Macy's Postmodern Goose

Avian ovulation
is a committed affair
the father to be
preening in plain sight
at the stop sign—
less friendly than other Canadians
he attacked
passersby
with a postmodern misplaced petulance.
He held no cardboard at this corner,
but stood guard as a sidewalk gargoyle
in this space
that to him, was clearly his.
Pedestrians jumped through the bushes
with Neiman Marcus bags
in the shadow of American Eagle,
ambushed by the ancient instinct
to protect one's own offspring.
This context lacked
the normal accouterments
for water fowl
mother warming eggs atop the mulch
behind the shrub
alongside Macy's.
He honked at the coming car
and flew at it
with murderous intent—

the driver stopped well before the sign
stunned.
Don Quixote's windmill charge
was less absurd
than a fourteen-pound bird
frantically flapping and charging
at 14 hundred pounds
of German engineering.

No pond nearby
the goslings webbed feet
will here be alien
in a land of pavement
and Prada.
Flying thousands of miles
with military precision in navigation
silly goose, why stop here?
in suburban opulence?
Maybe the eggs came
at the wrong time of month?
Were the better nesting sites taken?
Or did she like window shopping,
and envied life in the suburbs?
Or maybe
in some collective memory
there was once a pond
before cement and neon lights
and they migrated back
to this spot in an attempt
to return to that home

from which they, like us,
feel somehow exiled
and settle down to nest
becoming instead the
tragicomical emblem
of our own sense
of displacedness.

How different do we look,
flying at one another
with words
to defend
our fallen ideologies
that we cling to
to give us that sense of home?

The Smell of History

Would you have commissioned such
a pricey portrait bust of yourself
if you knew how
unkind time would be?
Disfigured
like Apache adulterers
forever frozen in art museums
staring—
seeing—
but never smelling
the years that pass you by.
Your likeness so less
likable without a nose.
Marbled into an artifact
you stand erect
explaining your position,
posh as it was, indefinitely.
But is it we, the extant observers,
who missed the smell
of the swell of apple orchards
or poison in your national accords?
Our olfactory ability
is not backward reading.
We can only see
the fractured artifacts you left,
and the words you victors collected.

I doubt the future will be more kind to us.
What do we know
of the noisy smell
of our nose-less Face-
books?
Marking out binary
representations of our own likenesses,
stone cold certainties, and successes,
in quips, and pics, and GIFs.
Lacking the depth of memory
or scent of togetherness,
stuffed in the smell
of roast turkey.

Dasein

Being human
means what exactly?
Other than that anthropologists
will someday unearth
our motivations
by assembling a collage of artifacts
from the winning societies
who were so kind (or arrogant enough)
to pollute for posterity.
A clever artifice to delineate
past societies contours
by generationally removed
dumpster diving.

Doctors might say being a human being
in being has something to do
with a heart that is beating
but there are those who have still voted
with an artificial pump.
Thus far, people have had parents
at least with an egg and a sperm
and a womb to be grown in.
Maybe while those future anthropologists
are digging up my dirty car
to determine the finer points
of ancient American civilization
doctors will sequence genes

with genetics writing gizmos
and *people* will be born entirely of tech.
What does it mean to be a noun,
and not a place or a thing?
Is it all manner of critters with mammaries
that need nurture and belonging?
I'm not sure chimps can yet sign *Modes Ponens*
or articulate a metaphysics.
Is it just the questions of being
or also those of justice
that separate us
from our tree swinging cousins
who don't investigate
the artifice of their ancestors
or their ethics?

Who is My Brother?
Written after waking up and having read T.S. Eliot's "The Hollow Men" the previous evening.

Are we really going around
this prickly-pear
so early in the morning
again?
If it is between the thing and its essence
that the shadow lies,
then where is its truth telling?
Between the past and the future
presents the lies of the shadow.
Epiphenomenal shading of noumena
by concurrent disassociation.
For Thine is the Kingdom
how can the hollow men
be also stuffed?
Who really does the skull-cracking
in death's midnight kingdom?
Is there a point to this prattling?
Do peonies prefer pragmatism to alchemy?
What is the magic magnetism that
opens the casing to reveal the brilliant petals
that get the bees buzzing?
Is it for those colors that the birds sing?
The spirit of the wind
moves through them
in between the shadow and the things.
In the thrush's whistle and the rustling thistle
is the spirit of the wind.

O Spirit, have mercy on us,
that like the forest, you not fire us
without severance pay.
Rather, like the apostles, blow on us
with your fire, O spirit,
that we might with joy face
the splitting end of Caesar's saw.
After Alexander saw, came, and conquered.

For Hecuba? What am I to Hecuba
or she to me that I should weep?
Should that my head be a fountain
that I should weep for the slain
of the daughter of those I thought were my people?
But they don't protest in the right manner
to be the same *ism*
and have a wrong shaped steeple.
Should I weep for the slain of the daughter
of the Syriac Christians?
Genocide isn't half bad if you don't know
at all about it.
Brother Thomas,
I doubted
you were my brother,
before your end at the sickle's edge
in the harvest
of a religion of peace.
The earth drank in your blood
so you are no longer walking or standing
for me to put my hand

in the hole in your side
and feel our kinship.
You, like me, bore a Christian name,
but where did the similarity start or stop?
Was it just a tenuous attachment
to a dusty footed Jew
who walked from Galilee proclaiming
a Kingdom we cannot see?

With Which of the Fives Senses Do You Feel Belonging?

*Why is loneliness not
A chemical discomfort,
Nor being a smell?* W.H. Auden

The world
goes mad on Wednesdays.
The other days too
it spins with a
dizzying intensity I cannot
calibrate my brain to track with.
Earth spins on its axis
circling the sun in an oval,
the sun is swirling in a galaxy
expanding.
Have you ever felt the unsettling waves
of your own electrons?
I have felt the swirling
of the hydrochloric acid
in my stomach
as it breaks down my hamburger
to become me.
I do not know what to do with
the perpetual impermanence
of being unmade and remade
from marmalade and toast and tea.
Memories being laid in the ever-shifting
bedrock
of the bedtime stories I tell myself

so I think the spinning
can make sense.
Sensory symphonies serenade me
with *quality qualia*
that I cannot un-perceive.
Meaning is imperceptible between
the fields of the five senses.
Waves of sound from nature
break against me and reverberate
through my vertebrae and bones
in my ears, but I do not hear
a sense of home.

When the world falls apart
into facts
data enacts no meaning.
What contiguity can
causal connections create?
Super fortresses flying
high above rooftops
ready to drop atomic
propositions,
exploded myths
and radioactively decaying truths
that cannot compete
with the desires
of youths
for the Real
for the Revolution,
a stream to swim in
that belongs to them.

Consciousness and Netflix
both streaming on
demand
the weight of the day
be lightened.
LED screens flashing across
the back of my brain
in an upside-down dilemma
of delineating
which things are stranger
and whether there is danger
in the spinning

until I, standing there,
see you
turning round
opening the windows
of your soul
with an honest intensity
toward me.
Your sonorous voice
warming the air
carrying kindness
and silencing the sense
of unsettling.
With the gentle touch
of your hand in mine,
meaning is manifest
and I am pulled fully
into this place and this time,

Out of the spinning
and into a knowing—
waves of feeling
reeling me towards you
inciting a deep sense
of belonging

Voiceless

I lost my voice to cancer
when I was 8 years old.
You might wonder how I had the time
by 8 to smoke enough cases of Camels,
but it wasn't Joe Camel
or the Marlborough Man
that took my voice.
It was Lymphoma
that locked up my larynx
and took away my breath.

Can you hear me?
Can you HEAR me?!?
Can you hear ME!?!

When I was two, my dad's spleen
weighed more than I did when I was born.
He was pregnant
with 10 pounds of poison.
When I was 6, he let my sister and I
pull the hair off his head
in chunks
fistfuls came out with
a tiny tug.

When I was 28, I was mortally afraid
that I would never
be seen.

Going to church for a potluck
was never quite like that one time,
when I was seven,
when blue pieces of paper were handed out
with my dad's picture on them.
A black and blue picture
with a smile big enough
to brighten any dark day.
I remember feeling proud and praiseworthy that day
that I too
had a smile on my face.
People I knew from far off places
like Wyoming and relatives from Oregon
had flown in for that particular potluck.
I don't remember what was on my plate,
but I do remember being actually happy
with better food than we normally ate.
If you smile and look strong,
people look at you with less pity.
And I want pity like I want Job's boils
or his friends for that matter.
Condescending, though well intended glances
made me feel like I was in the land of Lilliputians
powerless before the giant Gulliver called fate;
driving a wedge between me and all other people
making me feel that my troubles
are really all the more my own.
I don't like to feel worse myself by inconveniencing
other people with the trouble
of feeling a response to my pain.

Can you hear me?

It was 23 three years later that I realized the cost
of my holding it together then.
The day I found out
he died
my mom and aunt and Uncle
pulled me out of the last class
of my second week of second grade.
I remember crying
in the room where I had a pizza party
months later for good grades.
Maybe the smile I had the next week at that potluck
was more particularly evidence that by the time
I started second grade
I was already committed to not really feeling.
How can you really feel the ineffaceable loss
of one of the stalwarts of your upbringing
responsible for your survival and socialization at seven?
He taught me music and English
and probably in that order.
How is it that you learn to be human?
He wasn't exactly always the best of mirrors
to reflect my emotional states.
Chemotherapy isn't known to cause kindness.

Was it wrong to feel happy
with all the attention I got that day?
A lot of people really seemed to care,
if only for a few hours.

When funerals are the only family reunions
or vacations you have,
they became strangely celebratory
if only in my mind.

I'm grateful that before
His heart monitor went flat
my dad taught me to wonder.
He lifted me up to his shoulders to see wild flowers
in untamed mountain meadows.
In such a meadow with a horizon of mountain peaks,
the earth reclaimed his substance.
In an un-birth she opened her womb
and took back the fragments
of dust and shards of bone.
My beginning ended there
beneath a tree and a makeshift cross
of fallen branches to mark the place
his carbon composted into wildflower fodder.
Twenty years later I wandered around
fields and forests
trying to find that same spot where he lay,
or rather, where we had dumped a plastic bag
of bone shards and dust that bore his name.

I'm not sure if cancer
is more cruel than kids
who attack the weak to secure
their own sense of self
I didn't know I was poor

until they let me know
my knock-off Nikes
and thrift store shirts
came up short
in the commodity of coolness.
I thought all food was from food banks.
Fuzzy bread was broken
for broken me.

Who was there to tell when I ended up weeping
beneath the jungle-jim when the other kids
cheated at games?
My mother exhausted from care-giving to a chemo patient
had no space to hold.
There was no one to tell.
So I swallowed the shame.
I swallowed the pride
of an eight year old
who's dad just died.
I swallowed my outrage at an unjust world.
I swallowed the anger at the boys who lied
cheated and laughed to climb
the social ladder over top of me.
I retreated into the recesses of my mind.
I stomped on my tenderness
and despised my susceptibility to care
I hated my heart.
I reviled my tears.

The great wall is a small thing
compared to the walls I built.

I can't number the dreams that died in its construction.
But like the great wall, the Mongols
could always bribe a guard or find a weak point
and there still was no safety and even less peace.
It did not keep out pain or shame,
but it worked well to repel warmth and kindness.
The pain and shame and anger I swallowed
became an impenetrable obstacle
to the warmth of connection
If I didn't care, then I couldn't have
my desires despised
my dreams dealt away with
my hopes inhibited.

Each poem is a plea
for you to see that I exist,
there is breath in my lungs
and pounding in my chest
and sound locked in my throat.
It wasn't until I felt the flame of my life
near being extinguished near 30
that I realized I had had
no voice.

Can you hear me?

If you made it this far,
you're still listening.
You can—
hear—me.

Phillip Emanuel Frost Bounds is a poet, pilot, and a pundit for perplexity (with an emphasis on the pun). He is also an attorney, axe throwing coach, swing dancer, and intellectual adventurer with a penchant for precise word usage and an affinity for antinomies. He is a transplant from Colorado but is glad to call Kansas City home. He has a bachelor's degree in philosophy from the University of Colorado in Colorado Springs, and a Juris Doctorate from the University of Denver. You can find more of his writing online at ifbrevity.com or on Instagram at @ifbrevity_poetry.

www.ingramcontent.com/pod-product-compliance
Lightning Source LLC
Chambersburg PA
CBHW020124130526
44591CB00032B/517